ABBREVIATED PRESCRIBING INFORMATION

<u>Indications</u>: Tazocin is a broad spectrum bactericidal penicillin for the treatment of the following infections caused by sensitive bacteria:- lower respiratory tract infections, urinary tract infections, intra-abdominal infections, skin infections, septicaemia and polymicrobic intra-abdominal, skin and lower respiratory tract infections; patients with impaired host defences. <u>Dosage</u> (intravenous use only): *Adults/elderly/children over 12:* Usually 4.5g every 8 hours (range from 2.25-4.5g every 6-8 hours dependent on the severity). *Children:* No data to support use. *Renal Impairment:* Dosing reduction may be necessary, please consult data sheet. <u>Contra-indications</u>: Hypersensitivity to penicillin, cephalosporin or ß-lactamase inhibitors. <u>Warnings</u>: Discontinue if anaphylactic or allergic reaction occurs. <u>Precautions</u>: Periodic assessment of renal, hepatic and haematological function advised. Discontinue if bleeding manifestations occur. Resistant bacteria may cause superinfection. Convulsions may occur with higher than recommended doses. Possibility of hypokalaemia in patients with low potassium or on cytotoxics or diuretics. Evaluate patients for syphilis prior to treatment for gonorrhoea. <u>Use during pregnancy or lactation</u>: Only if benefit outweighs risk. <u>Side-effects</u>: Most frequent: gastro-intestinal disturbances; various skin reactions including rashes, erythema, pruritus and urticaria; allergic reactions; superinfection; phlebitis, thrombophlebitis, pain/inflammation at site of injection. Less frequent: muscle pain or weakness; hallucination; dry mouth; stomatitis, sweating; oedema; tiredness and rarely leucopenia, interstitial nephritis. Haematological changes, increases in liver and rarely renal function test values have been reported. <u>Overdose</u>: Piperacillin may be reduced by dialysis. <u>Presentation</u>: Tazocin 2.25g: Vials containing piperacillin 2g (as piperacillin sodium) and tazobactam 250mg (as tazobactam sodium). Tazocin 4.5g: Vials containing piperacillin 4g (as piperacillin sodium) and tazobactam 500mg (as tazobactam sodium). <u>Basic NHS Price</u>: 4.5g strength:- single vial £13.16, single infusion pack £14.48; 2.25g strength single vial £7.24. <u>PL nos</u>: 4.5g strength PL 0095/0254; 2.25g strength PL 0095/0252). <u>PA nos</u>: 4.5g vials 37/68/2; 4.5g combipack 37/68/3; 2.25g vial 37/68/1. <u>Legal Category</u>: POM. Further information is available on request from: Wyeth Laboratories, Huntercombe Lane South, Taplow, Maidenhead, Berks SL6 0PH. Tel (01628) 604377. Product Licence Holder: Cyanamid of Great Britain Limited, Cyanamid House, Fareham Road, Gosport, Hampshire, PO13 0AS. Date of preparation: June 1996. *Trade mark.

<u>REFERENCES</u>   1. Pallett AP. ICID, Prague 1994; Abstract 857. 2. Ravichandran D. Br J Surgery 1994; 81 (Suppl 1): 75. (102185) 3. Huizinga WKJ. 7th European Congress of Clinical Microbiology and Infectious Diseases, Vienna 1995: Abstract 573.

ZTAZ 421/0696

MCQs in
Microbiology and Infection
for the FRCS

MCQs
in
Microbiology and Infection
for the
FRCS

P. W. Ross TD, MD, FRCPath, FRCPE, CBiol, FIBiol, FLS
Reader in Medical Microbiology, University of Edinburgh
Honorary Consultant Bacteriologist, Royal Infirmary of Edinburgh NHS Trust
Examiner, Royal College of Pathologists and Royal College of Surgeons of Edinburgh

F. X. S. Emmanuel MB, BS, MSc, PhD, FRCPath
Consultant Bacteriologist, Royal Infirmary of Edinburgh NHS Trust
Honorary Senior Lecturer in Medical Microbiology, University of Edinburgh
Examiner, Royal College of Pathologists

with a Foreword by

Sir David C. Carter MD, FRCSE, FRCSG, FRCPE, FRSE
Regius Professor of Clinical Surgery, University of Edinburgh
Honorary Consultant Surgeon, Royal Infirmary of Edinburgh NHS Trust
Past Chairman, Scottish Council for Postgraduate Medical and Dental Education
Surgeon to HM the Queen in Scotland

 **PETROC PRESS**

Petroc Press, an imprint of LibraPharm Limited

Distributors

Plymbridge Distributors Limited, Plymbridge House, Estover Road, Plymouth PL6 7PZ, UK

Published in the United Kingdom by LibraPharm Limited, *Gemini House*, 162 Craven Road, Newbury, Berkshire RG14 5NR, UK

A catalogue record for this book is available from the British Library

ISBN 1 900603 15 2

Typeset by Richard Powell Editorial and Production Services, Basingstoke, Hampshire RG22 4TX
Printed and bound in the United Kingdom by Hartnolls Limited, Bodmin, Cornwall

Contents

Foreword

Infectious diseases remain a major cause of morbidity and mortality throughout the world. Success in some areas, such as the eradication of smallpox, have sadly to be balanced against new scourges such as HIV infection and AIDS, and by the recrudescence of diseases such as tuberculosis, which we mistakenly regarded as vanquished. Bacterial drug resistance now looms large as a continuing and increasing problem, underlining the need for the doctor of today to comprehend the issues concerned and operate rational policies of prevention and management of infection.

This excellent book consists of a series of multiple choice questions and answers and has been compiled by Drs Ross and Emmanuel primarily for those undertaking the postgraduate examinations held by our Royal Colleges of Surgery. The book is well suited to serve as an aid to learning during preparation for these examinations and the commentaries provided mean that it can also function as a learning test in its own right. Consultant surgeons also need to understand microbiology and the prevalence and treatment of infection. The new emphasis on continuing medical education means that this book may prove valuable to consultants as well as their trainees.

The success of the sister textbook, which was aimed at doctors preparing for the MRCP examination, testifies to the ability of books of this type to fulfil a need. The format employed has obviously proved popular. The production of a surgical edition now provides the surgical community with an up-to-date source of information which is at the advancing edge of the rapidly changing field of microbiology.

David Carter

Preface

MCQs are an increasingly important component of medical postgraduate examinations including those for Fellowship of the Royal College of Surgeons. This book, written to assist candidates to prepare for these, can be used either as an initial learning text or as a check of knowledge during the stages of revision.

Questions are in the true–false style, the format of the Fellowship MCQs. They are not grouped into body systems or topics that are related and the various sub-divisions of microbiology are not assembled separately because questions in the examination are not organised in this way. The book is divided into four sections, each of which contains a broad mix of questions and answers.

The answers provided also include appropriate commentary on the questions, so that the candidate's knowledge may be supplemented without repeated recourse to major textbooks.

Every effort has been made to cover a wide range of subjects in the various areas of microbiology and infection that are of relevance to surgery, to help to underpin the knowledge required by the surgeon in clinical practice as well as to provide information for the more immediate chore of passing examinations.

P.W.R.
F.X.S.E.

"Every operation in surgery is an experiment in bacteriology."
Lord Moynihan, 1920

Section 1   Questions

1. Triple vaccine for the prevention of virus infections protects against

A. mumps virus
B. coxsackie virus
C. measles virus
D. rubella virus
E. adenoviruses

2. Advantages of sterilisation by ionising radiation include

A. short sterilisation time
B. reliability of sterilisation
C. negligible rise in temperature
D. ability to sterilise equipment made of heat-sensitive materials, e.g. polystyrene
E. no deleterious effects on glassware or textile fibres

3. Tetanus toxoid

A. need not be given for superficial wounds
B. is given three times to babies as a component of triple vaccine
C. confers passive immunity
D. should be avoided in the immunocompromised person
E. administration within the last five years obviates the need to give antibiotics in a case of tetanus-prone injury

4. Ethylene oxide is the agent commonly used for the sterilisation of

A. fibre-optic endoscopes
B. glassware
C. rubber tubings and catheters
D. prosthetic cardiac valves
E. respiratory ventilators

5. *Enterococcus faecalis* is

A. a frequent cause of pyogenic infections
B. a Gram-negative coccus
C. usually sensitive to aminoglycosides
D. often resistant to cephalosporin antibiotics
E. associated with infection in hip prostheses

6. Methicillin-resistant *Staphylococcus aureus* (MRSA)

A. is usually sensitive to vancomycin
B. is more likely to cause deep-seated infection
C. is often resistant to many antistaphylococcal antibiotics
D. may cause asymptomatic colonisation
E. may be phage-typed for epidemiological purposes

7. Aminoglycoside antibiotics such as gentamicin

A. act on the bacterial cell wall
B. are active against staphylococci
C. are effective in the treatment of anaerobic myositis
D. are contra-indicated in patients with renal impairment
E. may cause loss of visual acuity in the elderly

8. In bacterial endocarditis

A. blood cultures may be negative
B. staphylococci are rare causative organisms
C. the inability to control infection with antibiotic therapy is an indication for replacement of the affected valve
D. combination therapy with a penicillin and an aminoglycoside is advised in most cases
E. cystoscopy is a predisposing factor

9. Rotavirus infections

A. are rare in adults
B. are diagnosed by stool culture
C. may present with colicky abdominal pain
D. often present with bloody diarrhoea
E. can easily be spread from person to person

10. Epididymo-orchitis

A. is associated with prostatitis
B. is a complication of gonococcal urethritis
C. is a manifestation of genital infection with *Ureaplasma* spp
D. occasionally complicates mumps
E. may be caused by *Mycobacterium tuberculosis*

11. The following vaccines contain living agents

A. BCG
B. oral polio
C. hepatitis B
D. diphtheria
E. yellow fever

12. The antistreptolysin O titre is raised in infections caused by

A. *Streptococcus sanguis*
B. *Streptococcus pneumoniae*
C. *Streptococcus pyogenes*
D. *Streptococcus bovis*
E. *Streptococcus mutans*

13. The following are causes of gas gangrene in man

A. *Clostridium histolyticum*
B. *Clostridium septicum*
C. *Clostridium novyi*
D. *Clostridium sporogenes*
E. *Clostridium perfringens*

14. Antibiotic prophylaxis for colonic surgery

A. has proved to be of clear benefit
B. should be started at least three days before surgery
C. should always include an antianaerobic agent such as metronidazole
D. depends on achieving adequate levels of antibiotics within the bowel
E. is used mainly for the prevention of tetanus and gas gangrene

15. The haemolytic uraemic syndrome

A. is more common in children
B. in the majority of cases is caused by infection with verotoxin-producing *Escherichia coli*
C. is rarely associated with haemorrhagic colitis
D. is caused by an infective agent that may be transmitted with food
E. may present as an acute abdomen

16. The following have oncogenic properties in humans

A. hepatitis B virus
B. papovaviruses
C. enteroviruses
D. measles virus
E. Epstein–Barr virus

17. Lyme disease

A. is spread by ticks that are parasitic on many mammals
B. is a multisystem disorder
C. is caused by *Borrelia burgdorferi*, a spirochaete
D. is diagnosed by serological tests
E. is confined to northern Europe

18. The following antimicrobial drugs are effective against penicillinase-producing staphylococci

A. ampicillin or amoxycillin
B. phenoxymethylpenicillin
C. cefuroxime
D. co-amoxiclav
E. cloxacillin

19. The following are spirochaetes which produce disease in man

A. *Trichinella spiralis*
B. *Borrelia vincenti*
C. *Treponema pertenue*
D. *Leptospira canicola*
E. *Borrelia burgdorferi*

20. Acute rheumatic fever is

A. a complication of infection of the throat by *Streptococcus pyogenes*
B. an indication for long term penicillin prophylaxis
C. rare in developed countries
D. prevented by immunisation
E. associated with positive blood cultures

21. In tuberculous infection of the urinary tract

A. the renal pelvis is most commonly affected
B. nephrectomy is usually necessary in addition to antituberculous chemotherapy
C. the demonstration of acid-fast bacilli in an early morning sample of urine is usually diagnostic
D. sterile pyuria is a consistent laboratory finding
E. *Mycobacterium tuberculosis* is the species most commonly involved

22. The following bacteria may be present in a person without causing infection in the host

A. *Clostridium difficile*
B. *Haemophilus influenzae*
C. β-haemolytic streptococci
D. *Clostridium perfringens*
E. *Salmonella typhi*

23. Disinfectants effective for skin application are

A. povidone-iodine solution
B. cetrimide
C. ethyl or isopropyl alcohol with povidone-iodine
D. glutaraldehyde
E. ethyl or isopropyl alcohol with chlorhexidine

24. Sterilisation by dry heat in the hot-air oven is indicated for the following

A. stainless steel surgical instruments
B. glass syringes
C. fabrics
D. cotton wool pledgets
E. paraffin gauze dressings

25. The following can be sterilised successfully in the autoclave

A. prosthetic heart valves
B. surgical instruments
C. talcum powder
D. petroleum jelly
E. fibre-optic endoscopes

26. The following may cause latent infections

A. cytomegalovirus (CMV)
B. *Bordetella pertussis*
C. herpes simplex virus
D. *Mycobacterium tuberculosis*
E. varicella-zoster virus

27. Endotoxins

A. may be secreted by Gram-positive bacteria
B. can be converted to a toxoid vaccine by formalin treatment
C. activate the complement system
D. are powerful inducers of antitoxic antibodies
E. are lipopolysaccharide molecules of which lipid A is the principal toxic factor

28. The diagnosis of pseudomembranous colitis (PMC) is aided by

A. colonoscopic biopsy of lesions
B. positive blood culture for *Clostridium difficile*
C. raised antibody levels in blood to *Clostridium difficile* toxin
D. isolation of *Clostridium difficile* from the stool
E. detection of *Clostridium difficile* toxin in the stool

29. Blood culture is commonly positive in the following infections

A. staphylococcal osteomyelitis
B. bacillary dysentery
C. typhoid fever
D. necrotising fasciitis
E. actinomycosis

30. Bacteria commonly causing serious lobar pneumonia following infection with influenza viruses are

A. *Streptococcus pyogenes*
B. *Streptococcus pneumoniae*
C. *Pseudomonas aeruginosa*
D. *Staphylococcus aureus*
E. *Haemophilus influenzae*

31. The following antibiotics act as inhibitors of cell wall synthesis

A. benzylpenicillin
B. cefuroxime
C. erythromycin
D. vancomycin
E. sulphonamides

32. Specific diagnosis of HIV infection can be made by

A. detection of viral antigens in the patient's blood
B. quantitation of CD4 lymphocytes in peripheral blood
C. isolation of the virus on culture
D. the presence of antibodies to HIV in the patient's serum
E. electron microscopy of the patient's serum

33. Primary peritonitis

A. has a predilection for patients with ascites
B. is often due to *Streptococcus pneumoniae*
C. is more common than secondary peritonitis
D. reveals foul-smelling pus at laparotomy
E. is an indication for treatment with penicillin

34. Examination of a "wet" film of urine can specifically identify

A. staphylococci
B. red blood cells
C. epithelial cells
D. white blood cells
E. mycobacteria

35. Gram-negative bacilli include

A. *Listeria* spp
B. *Lactobacillus* spp
C. *Proteus* spp
D. *Bacteroides* spp
E. *Pseudomonas* spp

36. Erythromycin is a first-line antibiotic in the treatment of infections caused by

A. *Mycoplasma pneumoniae*
B. *Chlamydia psittaci*
C. *Haemophilus influenzae*
D. *Legionella pneumophila*
E. *Neisseria meningitidis*

37. The following organisms causing infections in man may be acquired as a result of eating inadequately cooked meat

A. *Trichuris trichuria*
B. *Giardia lamblia*
C. *Toxoplasma gondii*
D. *Taenia saginata*
E. *Trichinella spiralis*

38. The Arthus reaction in man

A. is an acute inflammatory response
B. is due to localised antigen–antibody reaction
C. may occur after tetanus immunisation
D. occurs within half an hour of exposure
E. is mediated by IgE

39. Intestinal amoebae

A. commonly parasitise the jejunum and ileum
B. consist mostly of pathogenic species
C. may cause metastatic infection in the brain
D. are susceptible to metronidazole
E. are a common cause of cirrhosis of the liver in the tropics

40. Cell-mediated immune responses in the skin

A. usually take more than 48 hours to evolve
B. are important in the control of fungal infections of the skin
C. are characterised predominantly by monocytic cellular infiltration
D. can be diminished by corticosteroid treatment
E. include the tuberculin reaction

41. Bacteria commonly associated with the aetiology of septic shock are

A. *Escherichia coli*
B. *Neisseria meningitidis*
C. *Streptococcus pneumoniae*
D. *Staphylococcus aureus*
E. *Clostridium difficile*

42. Antimicrobial agents clinically useful against anaerobes are

A. gentamicin
B. clindamycin
C. chloramphenicol
D. metronidazole
E. ketoconazole

43. Micro-organisms recognised as transmissible by blood transfusion are

A. hepatitis A
B. *Mycobacterium tuberculosis*
C. HIV-1 and -2
D. cytomegalovirus
E. *Plasmodium vivax*

44. The following is/are true about *Helicobacter pylori*

A. it is a Gram-positive bacillus
B. it survives in the acidic environment of the stomach by producing a thick capsule
C. diagnosis of infection is usually made by histology of gastric biopsies
D. the majority of infected individuals will sooner or later develop duodenal or gastric ulceration
E. combination antibiotic therapy is indicated when infection is proven

45. Endotoxin can produce

A. circulatory collapse
B. leucopenia
C. disseminated intravascular coagulation (DIC)
D. fever
E. anaphylaxis

46. Hepatitis C virus (formerly one of the non-A, non-B hepatitis viruses)

A. is responsible for chronic liver disease in 50% of those infected
B. causes jaundice in a minority of infected persons
C. produces only mild symptoms
D. is an aetiological agent in hepatocellular carcinoma
E. is usually transmitted by arthropod vectors

47. Hepatitis A virus infection

A. has an incubation period of six to eight weeks
B. can be transmitted by sexual intercourse
C. often leads to chronic liver disease
D. confers long-lasting immunity
E. can be prevented by the use of killed vaccines

48. A raised titre of anti-HBs in the blood

A. signifies previous hepatitis B infection
B. is produced after hepatitis B vaccination
C. indicates immunity to hepatitis B infection
D. occurs during the incubation period of hepatitis B infection
E. indicates active hepatitis B infection

49. Useful drugs in fungal infections are

A. ribavirin
B. amantadine
C. fluconazole
D. idoxuridine
E. 5-flucytosine

50. The triple vaccine for the prevention of bacterial infections provides protection against infections caused by

A. *Haemophilus influenzae* type B
B. *Streptococcus pneumoniae*
C. *Bordetella pertussis*
D. *Neisseria meningitidis*
E. *Clostridium tetani*

Section 1   Answers

A1.
A. T
B. F   there is no effective vaccine against coxsackie viruses
C. T
D. T
E. F   as in B

A2.
A. T
B. T   for appropriate articles under controlled conditions
C. T
D. T
E. F   discoloration of glassware and loss of tensile strength in textile fibres

A3.
A. F   in susceptible individuals even superficial wounds may result in tetanus
B. T
C. F
D. F   tetanus toxoid is not a live vaccine and is safe in the immuno-compromised
E. F   antibiotics may be necessary to prevent other infections in contaminated wounds

A4.
A. F   though effective, the process of sterilisation with ethylene oxide is too long for routine use by endoscopy units
B. F   glassware is effectively and cheaply sterilised in the autoclave
C. T   expensive non-disposable heat-labile articles may be sterilised by this method
D. T
E. T   heat-labile components may be sterilised by this method

24

A5.
A. F   though it may occasionally cause intra-abdominal sepsis
B. F   they are Gram-positive cocci in short chains
C. F   MIC (minimum inhibitory concentration) against amino-glycosides is high and this organism would normally be considered to be resistant to aminoglycosides, but these antibiotics are sometimes used to treat infections with this organism in combination with penicillins because of synergistic action
D. T
E. T   though coagulase-negative staphylococcal species are the most common cause of infection in hip prostheses, enterococci are also significant pathogens in this situation

A6.
A. T
B. F   is no more likely to cause deep-seated infections than ordinary *Staphylococcus aureus* strains
C. T
D. T   many patients and staff exposed to MRSA may be colonised asymptomatically in the nose, axillae and groins
E. T   but other typing systems such as pulsed field gel electrophoresis may be more discriminating than phage typing in investigating the epidemiology of outbreaks.

A7.
A. F   act on ribosomes, so interfere with protein synthesis
B. T   though some strains may be resistant
C. F   have no activity against anaerobic organisms
D. F   can be used with caution and close monitoring of blood levels
E. F   neurotoxicity is to the vestibular and cochlear branches of the eighth cranial nerve

A8.

A. T some cases may be due to organisms such as *Coxiella*, *Chlamydia* and *Legionella*, which are difficult to culture on routine blood culture media

B. F staphylococci are often the cause of endocarditis, especially on prosthetic valves

C. T

D. T combination therapy is advised in cases where the causative organism is a streptococcus, enterococcus or staphylococcus, i.e. the vast majority of cases.

E. T particularly when infections are caused by enterococci

A9.

A. F less common than in children, but outbreaks of infection are not rare in adults

B. F this virus cannot be cultured; diagnosis is by detecting the virus by electron microscopy or by immunological methods

C. T but this symptom is an uncommon feature in rotavirus diarrhoea

D. F

E. T

A10.

A. T

B. T

C. F

D. T predominantly orchitis

E. T predominantly epididymitis

A11.

A. T

B. T

C. F this is a "component" vaccine, consisting of the surface antigen only

D. F this vaccine is composed of modified toxin (or toxoid)

E. T

A12.
A. F
B. F
C. T
D. F
E. F

A13.
A. T
B. T
C. T
D. F
E. T

A14.
A. T
B. F   usually commenced with induction of anaesthesia
C. T
D. F   tissue levels are more important
E. F   mainly used for the prevention of postoperative intraperitoneal or wound infection

A15.
A. T
B. T   the most common strain of verotoxin-producing *Escherichia coli* is O-157, but other serotypes of *Escherichia coli* may also produce the toxin
C. F   is commonly associated with colitis and bloody diarrhoea; this is the usual presentation in adults
D. T   but it is often difficult to isolate the organism from the food
E. T   haemorrhagic colitis with passage of blood and mucus and abdominal pain may occasionally be mistaken for a surgical emergency

A16.
A. T   associated with hepatocellular carcinoma
B. T   associated with genital tract malignancies
C. F
D. F
E. T   associated with Burkitt's lymphoma and nasopharyngeal carcinoma

A17.

A.   T   spread by many species of ixodid ("hard") ticks of many wild and domestic animals
B.   T   involves skin, joints, nervous system and cardiovascular system
C.   T   there is, however, much genetic variation in this organism
D.   T   though useful, serological tests have low sensitivity and are often falsely positive
E.   F   is widespread in north America, Europe and possibly elsewhere

A18.

A.   F   these agents are destroyed by the staphylococcal penicillinase (β-lactamase), which is produced by about 90% of all clinical isolates of *Staphylococcus aureus*
B.   F   as above
C.   T   cephalosporins are intrinsically resistant to the action of staphylococcal β-lactamase
D.   T   the clavulanic acid component of co-amoxiclav binds to and inactivates staphylococcal β-lactamase
E.   T   as in C

A19.

A.   T   causes trichinellosis, a myositis due to invasion of muscles by the larvae
B.   T   causes Vincent's angina
C.   T   causes yaws; this agent is similar to *Treponema pallidum*, the cause of syphilis
D.   T   one of the causative agents of Weil's disease (leptospirosis)
E.   T   causes Lyme disease

A20.

A.   T
B.   T   to prevent recurrence of throat infection with *Streptococcus pyogenes*
C.   T
D.   F   no vaccine available
E.   F   the streptococcal infection is confined to the throat

A21.
A. T
B. F standard antituberculous chemotherapy is usually sufficient
C. F urine samples often contain contaminating non-pathogenic *Mycobacteria* spp
D. T
E. T though in the past *Mycobacterium bovis* was also common; atypical mycobacterial species rarely cause renal infection

A22.
A. T particularly in the elderly and infants
B. T
C. T
D. T
E. T an asymptomatic carrier state and excretion of organisms may occur after recovery from typhoid

A23.
A. T
B. F antimicrobial activity is poor
C. T
D. F this agent is highly toxic and allergenic for use on the skin
E. T

A24.
A. F autoclave sterilisation is preferred
B. T
C. F
D. T steam penetration may be inadequate to guarantee sterilisation
E. F as in D

A25.
A. F these are presterilised by manufacturers using γ-irradiation
B. T
C. F steam penetration may be inadequate to guarantee sterilisation
D. F as in C
E. F these are heat-labile; immersion in glutaraldehyde or ethylene oxide treatment is preferred

A26.
A. T
B. F
C. T
D. T
E. T

A27.
A. F
B. F
C. T
D. F   though antibody response to endotoxins does occur, this is in-consistent and poorly protective
E. T

A28.
A. T   histology is pathognomonic
B. F   *Clostridium difficile* infection is not bacteraemic
C. F   antibody tests on blood are not of value in clinical diagnosis be-cause infection and toxin secretion are confined to the colonic lumen
D. T   but *Clostridium difficile* can also be isolated from the stool in some normal individuals, particularly children and the elderly
E. T   but *Clostridium difficile* toxin may also be present in the stool in some normal individuals

A29.
A. T
B. F   but bacillary dysentery may on rare occasions be bacteraemic
C. T
D. T   the causative organism is usually *Streptococcus pyogenes* (group A β-haemolytic streptococcus)
E. F   metastatic spread of infection may occur, but bacteraemia is rarely detected by blood culture

A30.

A. T

B. T   probably the most common cause of bacterial pneumonia secondary to viral influenza

C. F   rarely a cause of serious lobar pneumonia

D. T

E. F   though recognised (especially *Haemophilus influenzae* type B), this species is an uncommon cause of lobar pneumonia

A31.

A. T

B. T

C. F   acts by disruption of protein synthesis by binding to ribosomes

D. T

E. F   these inhibit folate synthesis

A32.

A. T   but this method is not commonly used

B. F   CD4 lymphocyte counts are low in patients with AIDS, but this does not provide a specific diagnosis

C. F   this is not part of the routine diagnostic tests

D. T

E. F

A33.

A. T

B. T   the other common pathogen is *Streptococcus pyogenes* (group A streptococcus)

C. F   primary peritonitis is a relatively rare condition

D. F   foul-smelling pus is a feature of faecal peritonitis

E. T   the two most common causative organisms are sensitive to penicillin

A34.

A. **F** though the presence of bacteria may be detected in a wet film of urine, their morphology would be indistinct; a Gram-stained film may give a better indication of bacterial morphology, but species identification and accurate quantification (viable counts) are possible only after culture

B. **T**

C. **T**

D. **T**

E. **F** Ziehl–Neelsen or auramine-phenol stain for acid-fast bacilli are necessary for the detection of mycobacteria

A35.

A. **F** Listeria are Gram-positive rods

B. **F** as in A

C. **T**

D. **T**

E. **T**

A36.

A. **T**

B. **T**

C. **F** many strains of *Haemophilus influenzae* are resistant to this antibiotic

D. **T** rifampicin may be added to erythromycin in serious cases

E. **F** the antibiotic of choice is penicillin

A37.

A. **F** the infection is usually spread by the faeco-oral route, due to poor personal hygiene

B. **F** infection is usually water-borne

C. **T** the cat is the primary reservoir, but transmission to humans often occurs through consumption of infected lamb, beef or pork

D. **T** this is the beef tapeworm

E. **T** causes trichinellosis, transmitted via pork

A38.

Note: The Arthus reaction is a localised antigen–antibody reaction at the site of introduction of antigen in individuals with high circulating levels of the corresponding antibody, e.g. local reaction to tetanus toxoid in individuals who are recently immunised; farmer's lung.

A.   T
B.   T
C.   T
D.   F   several hours to a few days
E.   F   IgG or IgM

A39.

A.   F   pathogenic amoebae mainly affect the colon (*Entamoeba histolytica*)
B.   F   most species are non-pathogenic, e.g. *Entamoeba coli*, *Entamoeba nana*
C.   T   though rare, this is an important complication of amoebiasis
D.   T   but cysts are not eradicated by metronidazole treatment; diloxanide furoate is advised to achieve eradication of cysts
E.   F   recovery from amoebic hepatitis is usually complete

A40.

A.   T
B.   T
C.   T
D.   T
E.   T

A41.

A.   T
B.   T
C.   T
D.   T
E.   F   the organism causes a mucosal infection in the colon, and causes localised cytotoxin-mediated damage, which may sometimes be quite severe

A42.

A. **F** aminoglycoside antibiotics such as gentamicin are inactive against anaerobic organisms
B. **T**
C. **T**
D. **T** metronidazole is the most consistent and potent agent against anaerobes
E. **F** ketoconazole is an antifungal agent

A43.

A. **F** hepatitis A is transmitted faeco-orally
B. **F** transmission is mainly airborne
C. **T**
D. **T**
E. **T** though rare, clearly documented cases have been reported

A44.

A. **F** this is a Gram-negative curved bacillus
B. **F** the ability to survive in the gastric environment is due to the production of a powerful urease enzyme, which breaks down urea to create an alkaline microenvironment
C. **F** the rapid urease test or culture are the tests most commonly used on biopsy material to establish specific diagnosis; non-invasive methods of diagnosis of infection are serology and the urea breath test
D. **F** though many people are infected, only a minority develop ulcers
E. **F** antibiotic treatment is indicated only when ulceration is present

A45.

A. **T**
B. **T**
C. **T**
D. **T**
E. **F**

A46.

A. T

B. T

C. T though initial symptoms are often mild, progressive liver damage is common

D. F hepatocellular carcinoma is associated with hepatitis B

E. F usually transmitted parenterally or by sexual contact, but transmission by insect bites is possible

A47.

A. F incubation period ranges from 15 to 45 days

B. F transmission is faeco-oral

C. F recovery is usually complete

D. T

E. T formalin-killed vaccine is available but immediate passive protection is provided by immune globulin

A48.

A. T

B. T

C. T

D. F

E. F

A49.

A. F this is an antiviral agent sometimes useful in treating respiratory syncytial virus infection

B. F this is an antiviral agent useful in immediate prophylaxis against influenza A infection

C. T useful for treating *Candida albicans* infections

D. F formerly used for treatment of herpes simplex virus infections

E. T broad spectrum antifungal agent usually used in combination with other antifungal agents, particularly amphotericin B

A50.

A. F this is available as a separate component vaccine, which is often given simultaneously with the triple vaccine
B. F
C. T
D. F
E. T

Note: The third component of the bacterial triple vaccine is *Corynebacterium diphtheriae* toxoid.

Section 2   Questions

51. In the investigation of the sources and transmission of outbreaks of hospital cross-infection with bacteria, the following typing methods may be useful

A. polymerase chain reaction (PCR)
B. enzyme-linked immunosorbent assay (ELISA)
C. bacteriophage susceptibility patterns
D. serotyping based on antigenic variation of cell-surface components
D. pattern of sensitivity to antibiotics

52. Viruses associated with arthritis include

A. hepatitis B
B. herpes simplex
C. rubella
D. parvovirus B19
E. papillomaviruses

53. Sterile arthritis following primary infection elsewhere in the body is associated with

A. *Yersinia enterocolitica*
B. *Clostridium difficile*
C. *Shigella* spp
D. *Streptococcus pneumoniae*
E. *Streptococcus pyogenes*

54. The following are true of acute osteomyelitis

A. it usually affects the shafts of long bones
B. trauma may be a predisposing factor
C. radiographic changes are diagnostic in the early stages
D. aspiration or drainage of pus is an essential part of management
E. benzylpenicillin is a good choice for initial therapy before bacteriological aetiology is established

55. In necrotising fasciitis

A. the most common pathogen is *Streptococcus pyogenes*
B. infection spreads rapidly along the plane between the dermis and the epidermis
C. appropriate antibiotic treatment alone is usually curative
D. blood cultures are usually positive
E. cases often occur in clusters

56. Candida albicans

A. infection is effectively treated with antimicrobial agents of the quinolone group
B. can be seen on Gram's stain
C. may be found as a commensal in the gut
D. can cause osteomyelitis
E. is a cause of oesophagitis

57. Bacteria associated with food poisoning are

A. *Helicobacter pylori*
B. *Clostridium perfringens*
C. *Staphylococcus aureus*
D. *Pseudomonas aeruginosa*
E. *Bacillus cereus*

58. Production of exotoxin is an important factor in the pathogenicity of

A. *Clostridium tetani*
B. *Klebsiella* spp
C. *Mycobacterium tuberculosis*
D. *Corynebacterium diphtheriae*
E. *Vibrio cholerae*

59. Water-borne infections include

A. poliomyelitis
B. schistosomiasis
C. typhoid fever
D. leptospirosis
E. cryptococcosis

60. Infection in prosthetic joint implants

A. is usually due to commensal skin organisms
B. takes several months to become clinically apparent
C. may be prevented by using systemic antibiotic prophylaxis during surgery
D. occurring during the operation is derived from the patient's skin in the majority of cases
E. is greatly reduced by the use of ultra clean laminar air-flow theatres

61. Conditions that significantly predispose to infective endocarditis include

A. atrial septal defects
B. mitral valve incompetence
C. coronary artery stenosis
D. diabetes mellitus
E. long-term central venous catheterisation

62. Postoperative hospital-acquired pneumonia

A. may be prevented by continued antibiotic prophylaxis in the postoperative period
B. is mainly due to cross-infection between patients
C. is a common cause of postoperative pyrexia
D. is reliably diagnosed by microscopy and culture of sputum samples
E. is often due to Gram-negative bacilli

63. Organisms of importance in causing pericarditis include

A. coxsackie viruses
B. *Mycobacterium tuberculosis*
C. *Escherichia coli*
D. *Entamoeba histolytica*
E. *Staphylococcus aureus*

64. Organisms commonly isolated from cardiac valve prostheses are

A. *Enterococcus* spp
B. *Mycoplasma* spp
C. *Staphylococcus epidermidis*
D. *Coxiella burneti*
E. *Acinetobacter* spp

65. Pseudomembranous colitis

A. is caused by *Clostridium perfringens*
B. is mediated by an exotoxin
C. is common in children
D. can result from hospital cross-infection
E. requires treatment with parenteral antibiotics in the acute stage

66. C-reactive protein (CRP)

A. is a non-specific serum protein
B. levels increase significantly in acute viral infections
C. is secreted by macrophages
D. levels may remain elevated for several weeks after eradication of infection
E. levels in health are less than 10 mg/litre

67. Pneumococcal vaccine

A. should be administered on an annual basis
B. is made from cell wall antigen from several serotypes
C. is given intradermally
D. is particularly important for persons who have chronic obstructive lung disease
E. is ineffective in splenectomised patients

68. The following virus infections are transmitted by the faeco-oral route

A. hepatitis A
B. hepatitis B
C. hepatitis C
D. hepatitis D
E. hepatitis E

69. *Pseudomonas aeruginosa*

A. frequently causes lung infection in patients with cystic fibrosis
B. is an important pathogen in chronic otitis media
C. produces exotoxins, which contribute to virulence
D. frequently causes septicaemia in patients with burns
E. is not sensitive to β-lactam antibiotics

70. *Enterococcus faecalis*

A. is a cause of infective endocarditis
B. is included in the common term "viridans streptococci"
C. is also known as *Streptococcus faecalis*
D. is highly susceptible to penicillin
E. may be resistant to vancomycin

71. Common causes of hospital-acquired pneumonia are

A. *Moraxella (Branhamella) catarrhalis*
B. *Klebsiella pneumoniae*
C. *Streptococcus pneumoniae*
D. *Mycobacterium tuberculosis*
E. respiratory syncytial virus (RSV)

72. The following are true of cerebral abscesses

A. temporal lobe abscess is often a complication of otitis media
B. antibiotic therapy alone is usually curative
C. they are a complication of infective endocarditis
D. infection is often due to more than one organism
E. the aetiological diagnosis is usually obtained by culture of CSF samples

73. The following are antibiotics useful for the treatment of surgical wound infection

A. cefuroxime
B. gentamicin
C. amoxycillin
D. teicoplanin
E. flucloxacillin

74. The laboratory should be alerted to infection risks (e.g. by marking the request form appropriately) when the following specimens are sent

A. urine sample from a patient with hepatitis B infection
B. blood sample from a patient with tuberculosis
C. wound drainage sample from a patient with hepatitis A infection
D. stool sample from a patient with AIDS
E. blood cultures from a patient with brucellosis

75. The following are true of methicillin-resistant *Staphylococcus aureus* (MRSA)

A. they are usually sensitive to aminoglycoside antibiotics
B. following operations on infected or colonised cases, operating theatres need to be thoroughly cleaned with disinfectants
C. they may be sensitive to the newer cephalosporins
D. they may be spread by airborne dust particles
E. they may be acquired in the community

76. Bacteria responsible for community-acquired pneumonia include

A. *Streptococcus pneumoniae*
B. *Legionella pneumophila*
C. *Staphylococcus aureus*
D. *Mycoplasma pneumoniae*
E. *Chlamydia trachomatis*

77. The following are examples of "prion" diseases

A. bovine spongiform encephalitis (BSE)
B. Jakob–Creutzfeldt disease
C. Burkitt's lymphoma
D. kuru
E. subacute sclerosing panencephalitis (SSPE)

78. Acute osteomyelitis

A. is usually caused by haematogenous spread
B. is most commonly caused by *Staphylococcus aureus*
C. is often associated with *Haemophilus influenzae* in children
D. frequently affects more than one bone
E. often yields positive blood cultures

79. *Pneumocystis carinii*

A. may cause cerebral abscess
B. may asymptomatically infect healthy adults
C. clinical infection is diagnosed by serological tests
D. produces disease mainly in patients with loss of T-cell immunity
E. may be isolated by blood culture using special mycological culture media

80. Cryptosporidiosis

A. is usually a self-limiting disease
B. may be acquired by person-to-person transmission
C. is usually an infection of immunocompromised patients
D. is diagnosed by detection of oocysts in the stool sample
E. may occur as water-borne outbreaks

81. Infections in which aminoglycoside antibiotics are often of value include

A. infective endocarditis
B. pyogenic meningitis
C. lobar pneumonia
D. hepatitis
E. cellulitis

82. The following are β-lactam antibiotics effective against *Pseudomonas aeruginosa*

A. ceftazidime
B. piperacillin
C. ciprofloxacin
D. gentamicin
E. co-amoxiclav

83. The following is/are true of infections associated with peripheral venous cannulation

A. they are often diagnosed by blood culture
B. they are usually due to Gram-negative bacilli
C. treatment is by injection of an appropriate antibiotic through the infected cannula
D. limiting the duration of cannulation is essential for prevention
E. they are more likely to occur in immunocompromised patients

84. Bacterial pathogens associated with sepsis in patients with burns include

A. *Proteus mirabilis*
B. *Staphylococcus epidermidis*
C. *Streptococcus pyogenes*
D. *Pseudomonas aeruginosa*
E. *Klebsiella* spp

85. Antibiotic prophylaxis is recommended for the following surgical procedures

A. mid-thigh amputation
B. vasectomy
C. resection of colon
D. urethral dilatation
E. haemorrhoidectomy

86. Acute gastroenteritis is a common manifestation of infection with the following

A. *Enterococcus faecalis*
B. ECHO virus
C. hepatitis A virus
D. *rotavirus*
E. *Cryptosporidium* spp

87. In human tuberculosis

A. *Mycobacterium bovis* may cause pulmonary disease
B. a killed vaccine is used to prevent disease
C. modern antibiotic treatment usually includes an aminoglycoside agent
D. *Mycobacterium avium-intracellulare* is a common cause in patients with AIDS
E. immunity is mainly due to humoral antibodies

88. *Staphylococcus aureus* **has a well established association with**

A. impetigo
B. cholecystitis
C. toxic shock syndrome
D. necrotising fasciitis
E. food poisoning

89. In enteric fever

A. more than one species of *Salmonella* may be implicated
B. perforation of the colon is a recognised complication
C. the carrier state may be eradicated by prolonged antibiotic therapy
D. blood cultures taken during the first week of illness are usually negative
E. prevention may be achieved by a live oral vaccine

90. *Streptococcus pneumoniae*

A. is a common aetiological agent in meningitis
B. is invariably sensitive to penicillin
C. infections can be prevented by vaccination
D. is a common cause of primary peritonitis
E. is frequently isolated in blood cultures from cases of lobar pneumonia

91. The following antibiotics should be used with caution in patients with renal failure

A. benzylpenicillin
B. metronidazole
C. gentamicin
D. cefuroxime
E. vancomycin

92. Penetrating injury with a needle that has been used for intravenous injection poses a risk to health care workers of infection with the following organisms

A. *Salmonella enteritidis*
B. hepatitis A virus
C. herpes simplex virus
D. *Clostridium difficile*
E. *Mycobacterium tuberculosis*

93. In tuberculosis

A. infection of the cervical lymph nodes should be treated with incision and drainage of any pus followed by antituberculous chemotherapy

B. patients with renal tuberculosis should be isolated during the first two weeks of chemotherapy

C. infection of the spine requires immobilisation in addition to chemotherapy

D. peritoneal involvement is usually secondary to perforation of a tuberculous lesion in the small bowel

E. blood cultures are useful in establishing an aetiological diagnosis

94. Coagulase-negative staphylococci

A. include all staphylococci other than *Staphylococcus aureus*

B. are a common cause of bone and joint infections

C. are often resistant to many commonly used antibiotics

D. colonise the skin of all people

E. are normally present in operating theatre air samples

95. Infections that are often caused by mixed bacterial pathogens include

A. cerebral abscesses

B. lobar pneumonia

C. peritonitis

D. liver abscesses

E. enteric fever

96. *Clostridium difficile*

A. may occasionally be found as part of the commensal flora of the gut

B. infection may require treatment with oral vancomycin

C. toxin, when detected in a stool sample, is pathognomonic of pseudomembranous colitis

D. is an obligate anaerobe

E. causes outbreaks of nosocomial (hospital acquired) infection

97. The following are aminoglycoside antibiotics

A. amikacin
B. streptomycin
C. clindamycin
D. gentamicin
E. vancomycin

98. In pyogenic liver abscess

A. jaundice is a common presenting feature
B. *Staphylococcus aureus* is a common pathogen
C. colonic pathology is often associated
D. blood cultures are often positive
E. prolonged antibiotics without drainage of pus are often curative

99. Infection with *Entamoeba histolytica*

A. usually affects the colon
B. is often asymptomatic
C. can usually be diagnosed by serological tests
D. is spread by the faeco-oral route
E. is eradicated by treatment with metronidazole

100. Barrier nursing is used to prevent hospital cross-infection in the following

A. legionellosis
B. methicillin-resistant *Staphylococcus aureus* (MRSA) infection
C. bacillary dysentery
D. tetanus
E. typhoid fever

Section 2   Answers

A51.
A. F this is not a typing method
B. F ELISA is often used to detect specific antigen or antibody, but not for typing
C. T commonly known as phage typing, useful with certain organisms such as *Staphylococcus aureus*
D. T e.g. capsular antigen typing of pneumococci
E. T this might often give an indication of strain identity, but is not sufficiently specific

A52.
A. T
B. F
C. T
D. T
E. F

A53.
A. T more common in patients who are HLA-B27 positive
B. F
C. T as in A
D. F arthritis may occasionally occur, but this is due to metastatic infection of the joint
E. T rheumatic fever arthritis may occur following streptococcal sore throat

A54.
A. F infection is usually adjacent to joints
B. T a history of preceding trauma at the site of the osteomyelitis is sometimes elicited
C. F radiographic changes may be minor or non-specific in the early stages
D. T if pus is present, it should be drained
E. F many pathogens that are important in acute osteomyelitis are often resistant to penicillin, e.g. *Staphylococcus aureus*

A55.
A. T this is by far the most important, though in some cases *Staphylococcus aureus* or anaerobes may also play a role
B. F infection spreads along the deep fascial planes
C. F identification of non-viable tissue and early wide excision is usually necessary in addition to antibiotic therapy
D. T
E. F most cases are sporadic

A56.
A. F these may predispose to candida infection
B. T
C. T but only in small numbers in healthy individuals
D. T candida osteomyelitis is a rare but important late complication of candida septicaemia
E. T

A57.
A. F though a common cause of infection in the stomach, this organism does not cause acute food poisoning
B. T associated with meat-based foods
C. T but uncommon; mediated by enterotoxins, which are secreted into the food
D. F though *Pseudomonas* spp may cause spoilage of food, they do not cause bacterial food poisoning
E. T associated with cooked rice; mediated by exotoxins secreted into the food

A58.
A. T the disease is due to the neurotoxin (tetanospasmin) secreted by the organism
B. F
C. F
D. T diphtheria toxin causes local tissue necrosis as well as systemic toxicity including myocardiotoxicity
E. T the powerful exotoxin (cholera toxin) inhibits reabsorption of water and electrolytes in the small bowel, leading to the severe watery diarrhoea and dehydration

A59.
A. T   by ingestion of faecally contaminated water
B. T   by contact with water infested with infected snails
C. T   as in A
D. T   by contact with water fouled by infected animals, e.g. rats
E. F

A60.
A. T   coagulase-negative staphylococci (i.e. not *Staphylococcus aureus*) are the most common infecting organisms
B. T
C. T   but efficacy is limited since the pathogens involved are often resistant to many antibiotics
D. F   though contamination may occur directly from the patient's skin, the more important source is contamination by airborne particles
E. T   but the reduction may not be marked, unless attention is also paid to all other aspects of theatre asepsis

A61.
A. F
B. T
C. F
D. F
E. T   usually right-sided endocarditis

A62.
A. F   prolonged use of antibiotics may predispose to pneumonia with antibiotic-resistant organisms
B. F   though cross-infection may occur, most cases are due to endogenous infection
C. T
D. F   organisms isolated from the sputum sample may only be those colonising the upper respiratory tract
E. T   though uncommon as primary pathogens in pneumonia, Gram-negative bacilli such as *Klebsiella* spp, *Pseudomonas* spp, etc. are important causes of postoperative pneumonia

A63.
A. **T**   especially coxsackie B virus
B. **T**
C. **F**
D. **T**   as an extension of liver abscess
E. **T**   as a complication of endocarditis

A64.
A. **T**
B. **F**
C. **T**
D. **F**   though well recognised, this is a rare cause
E. **F**   Gram-negative bacilli are uncommon causes of endocarditis of any type

A65.
A. **F**   caused by *Clostridium difficile*
B. **T**   mucosal damage is caused by a cytotoxin secreted by the organism
C. **F**   the disease is very rare in children, even though the organism may often be present in their gastrointestinal tract
D. **T**   this is a significant cause of serious hospital-acquired infection, particularly in wards with heavy antibiotic usage
E. **F**   oral antibiotics are preferred since the infection is confined to the colonic mucosa; vancomycin or metronidazole is given orally; the latter may be given parenterally in severe cases with toxic megacolon

A66.
A. **T**   it has no immunological specificity in its action
B. **F**   viral infections do not usually elicit a CRP response; bacterial infections often do
C. **F**   secreted by hepatocytes
D. **F**   levels fall rapidly on resolution of infection
E. **T**

A67.

A. F   once every five years is adequate; more frequent administration may result in painful local reactions

B. F   made from capsular polysaccharide antigen of the common serotypes

C. F   given intramuscularly

D. T

E. F   often effective in splenectomised patients; specific antibody levels may be measured in serum to confirm adequate response in doubtful cases

A68.

A. T
B. F
C. F
D. F
E. T

A69.

A. T   the mucoid forms are particularly difficult to treat; other pathogens involved in cystic fibrosis include *Staphyloccocus aureus, Haemophilus influenzae* and *Pseudomonas (Burkholderia) cepacia*

B. T

C. T

D. T   in general however, *Pseudomonas* septicaemias are more likely to occur in granulocytopenic patients

E. F   third generation cephalosporins and other β-lactam antibiotics such as piperacillin, azlocillin, etc. are active against most strains of *Pseudomonas aeruginosa*

A70.

A. T   particularly in the elderly

B. F   enterococci do not produce the partial (green) haemolysis characteristic of "viridans" streptococci

C. F   this term has been superseded by the current nomenclature

D. F   is generally much less susceptible than streptococci to penicillin

E. T   though still uncommon, multiply antibiotic-resistant enterococci (including resistance to vancomycin) are an emerging problem

A71.

A. T   especially in patients with pre-existing lung disease such as chronic obstructive airways disease

B. T   patients in intensive care are more susceptible

C. T   though most cases are community-acquired, hospital cross-infection does occur

D. F   hospital cross-infection with this organism is now rare

E. F   this is usually a community-acquired infection, though hospital outbreaks do occur

A72.

A. T

B. F   antibiotic treatment is essential but drainage of pus should not be delayed

C. T   but embolisation to the brain from cardiac vegetations often does not result in abscess formation

D. T   mixed aerobic and anaerobic infections are not uncommon

E. F   preferred sample for culture is pus from the abscess; CSF culture is often negative; blood cultures are often positive, but not all the organisms in a mixed infection may be isolated from the blood culture

A73.

A. T

B. F   most wound infections are caused by Gram-positive organisms such as *Staphylococcus aureus* or *Streptococcus pyogenes*, and aminoglycosides such as gentamicin are not the preferred antibiotics for these infections

C. F   most strains of *Staphylococcus aureus* are resistant to amoxycillin

D. F   though effective, other less toxic and less expensive antibiotics are available

E. T

A74.
A. T
B. F   *Mycobacterium tuberculosis* is rarely present in blood samples
C. F   hepatitis A virus is rarely present in tissues outside the gastro-intestinal system and is usually transmitted by the faeco-oral route
D. T
E. T   cultures of *Brucella* spp are highly infectious

A75.
A. F   many strains are multiply resistant, including resistance to aminoglycosides
B. F   thorough cleaning using detergents is sufficient
C. F   MRSA are always resistant to cephalosporins
D. T   though contact spread via the hands of medical and nursing staff is the most important route
E. T   though less prevalent than within hospitals, carriage of MRSA strains and their spread does occur in the community

A76.
A. T   the most common cause of lobar pneumonia
B. T   an uncommon but important cause
C. T   particularly as secondary bacterial infection in patients with viral respiratory tract infections such as influenza
D. T   another common cause
E. F   *Chlamydia trachomatis*, though a rare cause of hospital-acquired pneumonia in neonates, is not a significant cause of community-acquired pneumonia; however, *Chlamydia pneumoniae*, a newly recognised organism, is increasingly shown to be a cause of community-acquired pneumonia.

A77.
Note: "Prion" diseases are thought to be due to a self-replicating protein agent(s) that lack(s) DNA or RNA. Pathologically, they present as slowly developing but fatal spongiform encephalitis.
A. T
B. T
C. F   this is associated with Epstein–Barr virus infection
D. T
E. F   this is a complication of measles

A78.
A. T
B. T
C. T *Haemophilus influenzae* type B is an important cause in children aged up to four years, though the incidence is rapidly decreasing in countries where vaccination with HIB vaccine is common
D. F frequently affects only one bone, but dissemination due to septicaemia to other sites, including bone, and to adjacent joints may occur if treatment is delayed
E. T blood culture is nearly always positive

A79.
A. F
B. T it is uncommon, however, to find the organism in sputum samples from healthy individuals
C. F antibodies are frequently found in normal persons, and many immunocompromised patients who are infected may not produce an antibody response
D. T
E. F diagnosis is usually by visualisation of the organism in respiratory secretions, e.g. by direct immunofluorescence

A80.
A. T cryptosporidiosis is usually a self-limiting disease in normal people; however, in the severely immunocompromised, such as those with AIDS, it causes an intractable diarrhoea
B. T person-to-person transmission may occur during outbreaks, particularly among young children or within families
C. F healthy children and adults are often infected, but infection is more severe in the immunocompromised
D. T modified acid-fast stain is commonly used to detect the oocysts
E. T the organism is resistant to water chlorination

A81.
A. **T**   in synergistic combination with a penicillin
B. **F**   though the aminoglycosides are not the preferred antibiotics against the common pathogens in pyogenic meningitis, they may be used in some cases, e.g. neonatal meningitis due to Gram-negative bacilli
C. **F**
D. **F**   hepatitis is usually of viral aetiology
E. **F**   cellulitis is usually due to *Streptococcus pyogenes* or *Staphylococcus aureus*; aminoglycosides are not the preferred antibiotics against these organisms

A82.
A. **T**
B. **T**
C. **F**   though effective, this is a quinolone antibiotic
D. **F**   though this is effective against *Pseudomonas* spp, it is an aminoglycoside antibiotic
E. **F**

A83.
A. **T**
B. **F**   the most common colonisers of intravenous lines are staphylococci; colonisation with Gram-negative organisms may occur, but less frequently
C. **F**   the infected line must be removed
D. **T**   peripheral venous lines should not normally be left *in situ* for longer than 48 hours
E. **F**   all patients are at risk

A84.
A. **F**   though it may superficially colonise burns, invasive infection is uncommon
B. **F**   as in A
C. **T**
D. **T**
E. **F**   as in A

A85.
A. T penicillin prophylaxis is recommended to prevent clostridial infection
B. F
C. T metronidazole is recommended to prevent anaerobic infection
D. F unless the patient is at risk of endocarditis
E. F as in D

A86.
A. F this is a commensal organism in the gut
B. F
C. F
D. T
E. T

A87.
A. T
B. F BCG is a live vaccine, an attenuated strain of bovine tuberculosis (bacille Calmette–Guérin)
C. F aminoglycoside agents such as streptomycin are rarely used now, except for the treatment of some resistant strains
D. F infection with *Mycobacterium avium-intracellulare*, an atypical mycobacterium species, is common in patients with AIDS, but the disease is not called tuberculosis
E. F immunity is mainly cell-mediated

A88.
A. T *Streptococcus pyogenes* and *Staphylococcus aureus* are the causes of this superficial pustular skin infection
B. F cholecystitis is usually caused by gut commensals such as coliforms and enterococci
C. T mediated by an exotoxin, the toxic shock syndrome toxin (TSST 1), which is produced by some strains of *Staphylococcus aureus*
D. F the primary pathogen in necrotising fasciitis is usually *Streptococcus pyogenes*
E. T mediated by enterotoxins produced by some strains of *Staphylococcus aureus*

A89.

A. T   typhoid fever itself is caused only by *Salmonella typhi*; other "enteric fevers" may be caused by species such as *Salmonella paratyphi* A or *Salmonella paratyphi* B

B. T   perforation, usually in the ileum, or haemorrhage are recognised surgical complications of enteric fever

C. T   the carrier state may be eradicated in some cases by prolonged treatment with antimicrobial agents such as ciprofloxacin

D. F   blood culture is a useful investigation at all stages of enteric fever

E. T   this new vaccine, using the bio-engineered strain TY21a, is as effective as the killed parenteral vaccine

A90.

A. T

B. F   the majority of strains are very sensitive to penicillin, but resistant strains are emerging in many parts of the world

C. T   the vaccine contains the capsular polysaccharide from 23 of the more common serotypes of *Streptococcus pneumoniae*

D. T

E. T

A91.

A. F   but very large doses over prolonged periods may cause toxicity

B. F

C. T   but usage with careful monitoring of levels may be clinically indicated in some patients with renal failure

D. F   as in A

E. T   as in C

A92.

A. F   this is mainly a food-borne infection

B. F   this infection is transmitted mainly by the faeco-oral route

C. F   transmission is mainly by physical contact with infected individuals

D. F   infection is acquired by ingestion of the spores of the organism

E. F   the organism is rarely present in blood; infection is usually acquired by inhalation

A93.

A. F chemotherapy alone is usually sufficient

B. F this is true only of direct smear-positive cases of pulmonary tuberculosis

C. F immobilisation is unnecessary except when there is risk of instability and injury to the spinal cord

D. F peritoneal involvement is usually secondary to miliary (i.e. disseminated blood-borne spread) tuberculosis

E. F except in severely immunocompromised patients, detectable bacteraemia is uncommon

A94.

A. T

B. F but they are important causes of infection in prosthetic joint implants

C. T antibiotic resistance patterns are variable, but they are often more resistant than *Staphylococcus aureus* strains

D. T

E. T these are constantly shed from the skin of personnel in operating theatres and will be present in particles in the air unless the theatre is fitted with ultra-clean laminar flow systems

A95.

A. T often including anaerobes

B. F

C. T peritonitis is usually secondary to bowel perforation and therefore faecal organisms including anaerobes are involved; primary peritonitis, which occurs much less commonly, is usually due to a single pathogen such as *Streptococcus pneumoniae* or *Streptococcus pyogenes*

D. T

E. F due to a single *Salmonella* species such as *Salmonella typhi*, *Salmonella paratyphi* A, or *Salmonella paratyphi* B

A96.

A. T this is particularly true in infants and in the elderly

B. T metronidazole is an alternative

C. F toxins may only occasionally be present in stool samples in asymptomatic persons

D. T

E. T

A97.
A. T
B. T
C. F   clindamycin belongs to the macrolide group of antibiotics which includes erythomycin
D. T
E. F   vancomycin is a cell wall antibiotic useful for treating infection with resistant Gram-positive organisms such as methicillin-resistant staphylococci or resistant enterococci

A98.
A. F   jaundice is rarely a presenting feature in pyogenic liver abscess; the most common presentation is as pyrexia of unknown origin (PUO)
B. F   infection is often due to multiple pathogens, commonly including *Streptococcus milleri*, coliform organisms and anaerobes; *Staphylococcus aureus* is uncommon
C. T   colonic diseases associated with pyogenic liver abscess include diverticulosis, malignancy, Crohn's disease, ulcerative colitis and ischaemia
D. T   blood cultures are very useful in enabling the isolation of pathogens, but in mixed infections not all pathogens may be detected in the blood culture
E. T   aspiration of pus is necessary only for diagnostic purposes in most cases

A99.
A. T   but spread may occur to the liver and, less commonly, to other sites such as the brain to cause abscesses
B. T   particularly in endemic areas
C. F   serological tests are only useful in invasive disease such as liver abscess
D. T
E. T   but to eliminate carriage of cysts, treatment with furamide (diloxanide furoate) is also necessary

A100.

A. F   person-to-person transmission has not been described; spread is by inhalation of aerosols from contaminated water

B. T

C. T

D. F   patients with tetanus are not a source of infection to others

E. T

Section 3   Questions

101. Airborne spread is important in

A. meningococcal meningitis
B. *Staphylococcus aureus* infection
C. aspergillosis
D. hepatitis B infection
E. tuberculosis

102. *Escherichia coli*

A. is an important cause of glomerulonephritis
B. is often a cause of wound infections
C. causes traveller's diarrhoea
D. causes pyogenic meningitis
E. is the predominant bacterial species in the large bowel

103. Streptococcal infection of surgical wounds

A. is often associated with cellulitis
B. is best treated with aminoglycosides such as gentamicin
C. often indicates poor infection control procedures
D. may be associated with the toxic shock syndrome
E. diagnosis is usually confirmed by rising antistreptolysin O (ASO) titres

104. Pyogenic infections of the breast

A. usually present as abscesses
B. are usually due to *Staphylococcus aureus*
C. are more common during pregnancy
D. are adequately treated with penicillinase-resistant penicillins such as flucloxacillin
E. may be an early indication of a duct obstructing lesion such as a carcinoma

105. Infections due to non-sporing anaerobes such as *Bacteroides* spp or fusiforms

A. are usually due to hospital cross-infection
B. may be prevented by prophylactic antibiotic treatment
C. are a common complication in orthopaedic surgery
D. are adequately treated by a broad spectrum β-lactam antibiotic such as co-amoxiclav
E. are a cause of pseudomembranous colitis

106. Hydatid cysts

A. mainly affect the liver
B. are due to a zoonotic infection
C. are aetiologically diagnosed by the demonstration of cysts in stool samples
D. require urgent surgical removal to prevent spread to other organs
E. are rarely seen outside tropical countries

107. Metronidazole is effective against

A. *Giardia lamblia*
B. *Trichomonas vaginalis*
C. *Entamoeba histolytica*
D. *Cryptosporidium* spp
E. *Bacteroides fragilis*

108. *Chlamydia trachomatis*

A. is an obligate intracellular organism
B. is a common cause of pelvic inflammatory disease
C. infection is usually diagnosed by serological tests
D. is sensitive to antibiotics such as erythromycin or clarithromycin
E. can cause pneumonia in infants

109. *Pasteurella multocida*

A. mainly infects immunocompromised patients
B. is associated with animal bites
C. may cause rapidly progressing cellulitis and septicaemia
D. is sensitive to penicillin
E. infection can be prevented by immunisation

110. The following are common causes of urinary tract infection (UTI)

A. *Enterococcus faecalis*
B. *Pseudomonas aeruginosa*
C. *Proteus mirabilis*
D. *Escherichia coli*
E. *Candida albicans*

111. In schistosomiasis

A. characteristic ova may be seen by microscopy of stool samples
B. haematuria is a presenting feature
C. serology is not of value as a diagnostic method
D. the infective larvae are present in faecally contaminated soil
E. treatment with antiparasitic agents is usually effective

112. Micro-organisms causing chronic skin ulceration include

A. *Mycobacterium tuberculosis*
B. *Corynebacterium diphtheriae*
C. *Leishmania donovani*
D. *Staphylococcus aureus*
E. papillomaviruses

113. Splenic enlargement may be a feature of

A. staphylococcal septicaemia
B. schistosomiasis
C. enteric fever
D. cytomegalovirus infection
E. tuberculosis

114. Micro-organisms that cause acute obstruction of the upper airways include

A. influenza viruses
B. *Haemophilus influenzae*
C. anaerobic cocci
D. *Corynebacterium diphtheriae*
E. *Candida albicans*

115. *Pseudomonas aeruginosa*

A. is a Gram-negative bacillus
B. is a cause of cellulitis
C. causes chronic osteomyelitis
D. survives in hospital environments because of its resistance to drying
E. is sensitive to vancomycin

116. Monitoring of blood levels of the antibiotic is essential during treatment with

A. cefotaxime
B. vancomycin
C. chloramphenicol
D. gentamicin
E. acyclovir

117. Pyogenic lung abscess

A. may occur as a complication of pneumococcal lobar pneumonia
B. often requires surgical drainage in addition to antibiotics
C. when multiple, usually indicates staphylococcal sepsis
D. often follows aspiration pneumonia
E. may be a presenting feature in bronchial carcinoma

118. Acute cholangitis

A. may occur as a complication of biliary obstruction
B. is commonly due to coliform organisms
C. often leads to septicaemia and positive blood culture
D. is adequately treated with ampicillin alone
E. may lead to multiple abscess formation in the liver

119. Bacterial pathogens that cause concern because of their increasing resistance to antimicrobial agents are

A. *Streptococcus pyogenes*
B. *Streptococcus pneumoniae*
C. *Salmonella typhi*
D. *Neisseria meningitidis*
E. *Mycobacterium tuberculosis*

120. Herpes simplex virus

A. is reliably sensitive to acyclovir
B. consists only of one type
C. is sexually transmitted
D. is an RNA virus
E. is a cause of congenital abnormalities

121. *Yersinia pestis*

A. causes bubonic plague
B. may cause pneumonic plague
C. is primarily a pathogen of rodents
D. is transmitted by ticks
E. has been eradicated from most countries

122. Organisms that cause pyogenic infections in skeletal muscle include

A. *Staphylococcus aureus*
B. *Trichinella spiralis*
C. *Salmonella typhi*
D. varicella-zoster virus
E. *Leptospira* spp

123. The polymerase chain reaction (PCR)

A. is a sensitive test for the detection of specific antibodies in tissues and body fluids
B. enables results to be obtained within one hour of samples arriving in the laboratory
C. may be used for the detection of specific bacterial or viral DNA
D. is only effective when viable organisms are present
E. is not suitable for routine diagnostic use

124. Organisms associated with acute infective colitis include

A. *Escherichia coli* O-157
B. *Salmonella typhi*
C. *Clostridium difficile*
D. *Shigella dysenteriae*
E. *Entamoeba coli*

125. HIV is reliably inactivated by

A. the autoclave
B. the hot air oven
C. chlorhexidine
D. glutaraldehyde
E. hypochlorites

126. If isolated from a patient, the following are always associated with active infection

A. *Staphylococcus aureus* from nasal swabs
B. cytomegalovirus from a throat swab
C. *Clostridium difficile* from stools
D. *Mycobacterium tuberculosis* from sputum samples
E. *Entamoeba histolytica* cysts from stools

127. γ-Irradiation can be used to sterilise

A. glassware
B. saline for injection
C. disposable needles and syringes
D. latex catheters
E. theatre linen

128. Factors affecting the performance of a disinfectant are

A. pH
B. temperature
C. number of organisms present
D. concentration of disinfectant
E. type of organisms

129. A patient recently returned from west Africa is admitted with fever and a petechial rash

A. the differential diagnosis includes viral haemorrhagic fever (VHF)
B. a blood film examination for malaria parasites should be requested
C. blood cultures should be taken and processed without delay
D. all samples should be clearly marked to indicate a high risk of infection
E. the patient should be isolated

130. Oesophagitis due to infective causes

A. is more common in immunocompromised patients
B. may be due to yeast infection
C. is often part of disseminated infection
D. leads to oesophageal rupture
E. may be diagnosed by radiological examination

131. Erysipelas

A. is characterised by a red rash with raised, sharp edges
B. is more common in the elderly
C. may be caused by dermatophyte fungi
D. often involves the face
E. is confined to the distribution of a single nerve

132. In tetanus

A. diagnosis is made by isolation of the organism from infected wounds
B. the toxin is spread from the site of infection via the blood
C. death is often caused by cardiovascular instability
D. human antitetanus globulin is useful in prophylaxis
E. the causative organism is always sensitive to penicillin

133. Acute painful swelling of the thyroid

A. may be due to a pyogenic abscess
B. can be caused by viral infection
C. may be associated with hyperthyroidism
D. is an indication for blood culture
E. may be due to Hashimoto's disease

134. Bacterial spores

A. are killed by a temperature of 120°C for 20 minutes
B. can be stained by Gram's method
C. multiply in adverse environments
D. are resistant to antibiotics
E. are formed mainly by Gram-positive bacilli

135. Bacterial plasmids

A. are extrachromosomal genetic elements
B. may code for bacterial virulence factors
C. are important in the spread of resistance to antibiotics
D. may be transmissible among different species of bacteria
E. are usually composed of RNA

136. *Giardia lamblia* infection

A. may be diagnosed by serological tests
B. is caused by ingestion of cysts
C. may be spread by the respiratory route
D. affects mainly the ileocaecal region
E. may cause malabsorption syndrome

137. Medically important protozoa are

A. *Leishmania donovani*
B. *Schistosoma mansoni*
C. *Trypanosoma cruzi*
D. *Echinococcus granulosus*
E. *Toxoplasma gondii*

138. *Helicobacter pylori*

A. rarely infects people in developed countries
B. is transmitted with food or drinking water
C. may be identified by its production of urease
D. is associated with duodenal ulcers
E. infection can be eradicated by antibiotics

139. Organisms associated with atypical pneumonia are

A. *Haemophilus influenzae*
B. *Chlamydia psittaci*
C. *Mycoplasma hominis*
D. *Chlamydia pneumoniae*
E. influenza viruses

140. Unilateral acute swelling of the parotid gland

A. is usually associated with mumps
B. often indicates pyogenic infection
C. may be associated with parotid duct obstruction
D. is an indication for antibiotic therapy
E. may be associated with malignancy

141. *Chlamydia* spp are associated with the following infections

A. acute salpingitis
B. community-acquired pneumonia in adults
C. conjunctivitis
D. gastritis and peptic ulceration
E. lymphogranuloma venereum

142. Infection in ventriculoperitoneal shunts for hydrocephalus

A. is often due to Gram-negative organisms
B. is associated with nephritis
C. may present as persistent pyrexia
D. often necessitates the removal of the shunt
E. is associated with ventriculitis

143. Disseminated candidiasis

A. is usually due to *Candida* spp other than *Candida albicans*
B. is most often diagnosed by positive blood cultures
C. may be complicated by osteomyelitis
D. is associated with neutropenia
E. is a complication of broad spectrum antibiotic therapy

144. Broad spectrum antibiotic cover with a combination of antibiotics is indicated in

A. pyogenic liver abscess
B. peritonitis secondary to colonic perforation
C. pneumococcal pneumonia
D. primary peritonitis
E. surgical prophylaxis for prosthetic hip implants

145. *Corynebacterium diphtheriae*

A. causes infection in myocardial tissue
B. is transmitted by droplet spread
C. may cause skin ulcers
D. always produces the exotoxin (diphtheria toxin)
E. infection is reliably diagnosed by examination of the Albert's stained preparations of the swab of the pharyngeal pseudomembrane

146. Bacteria commonly causing sepsis in burns include

A. *Streptococcus pyogenes*
B. *Clostridium perfringens*
C. *Staphylococcus aureus*
D. *Bacteroides melaninogenicus*
E. *Pseudomonas aeruginosa*

147. Plantar warts

A. are caused by papillomaviruses
B. infect subcutaneous cells in the soles of the feet
C. elicit strong cell-mediated immunity
D. may lead to malignant epithelial neoplasms
E. are contagious

148. *Streptococcus pneumoniae* is associated with

A. pyogenic arthritis
B. brain abscess
C. endocarditis
D. empyema
E. hospital cross-infection

149. Antibiotics with activity against *Pseudomonas* spp include

A. azlocillin
B. gentamicin
C. cefuroxime
D. vancomycin
E. ciprofloxacin

150. *Escherichia coli*

A. is commonly associated with urinary tract infection
B. is the predominant organism in the colon
C. is often considered a contaminant when isolated from blood cultures
D. may be associated with meningitis
E. can cause severe haemorrhagic colitis

Section 3 Answers

A101.
A. **T**
B. **T** direct person-to-person spread by contact is also important
C. **T** the spores are spread by the airborne route
D. **F** hepatitis B is transmitted by inoculation of blood or body fluids
E. **T**

A102.
A. **F** it is a cause of acute or recurrent pyelonephritis
B. **F** though sometimes isolated from wound swabs, it is usually present only as a colonising organism
C. **T** due to enterotoxigenic strains newly acquired during travel
D. **T** particularly in neonates
E. **F** though the predominant aerobic species in the large bowel, anaerobes are by far the most numerous

A103.
A. **T**
B. **F** all streptococci are innately resistant to aminoglycosides
C. **T**
D. **F** though some strains of *Streptococcus pyogenes* can produce exotoxins that produce a shock-like syndrome, the classical toxic shock syndrome is associated with *Staphylococcus aureus*
E. **F** though this method may occasionally be used to confirm streptococcal infection in retrospect, the usual method is culture of wound swabs

A104.
A. **T** but some may present at an early stage as cellulitis
B. **T** anaerobes may also be involved
C. **F** more common postpartum
D. **T**
E. **F**

A105.

A. F   these are usually endogenous infections
B. T   metronidazole prophylaxis is effective
C. F
D. F   see B
E. F   pseudomembranous colitis is caused by toxigenic strains of *Clostridium difficile*

A106.

A. T   but many other organs, such as the lung, may also be affected
B. T   the causative tapeworm, *Echinococcus granulosus*, is a primary pathogen of many carnivores
C. F   daughter cysts are demonstrable in the hydatid cyst fluid, but do not reach the gut in man
D. F   surgery is not required unless the cyst causes complications as a space-occupying lesion
E. F   this disease is of world-wide distribution

A107.

A. T
B. T
C. T
D. F   there are no effective antibiotics for the treatment of *Cryptosporidium* infections
E. T   *Bacteroides fragilis* is an obligate anaerobe commonly involved in anaerobic sepsis

A108.

A. T
B. T   serotypes D–K are involved
C. F   detection of antigen or cultures from the infected site is the reliable method of diagnosis in individual cases; serology is useful in epidemiological studies
D. T   alternative therapy is tetracycline
E. T   acquired perinatally from infected mothers

A109.
A. **F** but infection may be more severe in the immunocompromised
B. **T**
C. **T**
D. **T**
E. **F** no vaccine is available

A110.
A. **T**
B. **T** particularly in catheterised patients or in those with abnormalities of the urinary tract
C. **T** particularly in children
D. **T** *Escherichia coli* is the most common cause
E. **F** but may cause infections in patients with indwelling catheters

A111.
A. **T** ova may also be detected in urine (particularly with *Schistoma haematobium*) or in rectal biopsy samples
B. **T** particularly with *Schistoma haematobium*
C. **F** an ELISA test for antibodies to ova in tissues is valuable in diagnosis
D. **F** infective larvae are present in water infested with the snails that are essential to the life cycle of schistosomes; these larvae enter the body by skin penetration
E. **T** agents such as praziquantel are effective

A112.
A. **T** this is rarely seen (and then as a result of accidental inoculation); other mycobacterial species such as *Mycobacterium ulcerans* or *Mycobacterium marinum* are more common as causes of skin ulcers
B. **T** a rare but important form of infection with *Corynebacterium diphtheriae*
C. **T** also known as cutaneous leishmaniasis
D. **F** staphylococcal skin infections are usually acute
E. **F** these produce warts, not ulcers

A113.

A. F
B. T   due to portal hypertension in long-standing schistosomiasis
C. T
D. T   particularly in congenital infections
E. F

A114.

A. F   but parainfluenza viruses are a common cause of croup in children
B. T   *Haemophilus influenzae* type B is the most common cause of acute epiglottitis
C. F   but other anaerobic species, such as Vincent's organisms and *Bacteroides* spp, may cause acute oedematous infection of the oropharynx
D. T   the pseudomembrane in diphtheria may cause laryngeal obstruction
E. F

A115.

A. T
B. F
C. T   primary osteomyelitis due to this organism is very rare, but chronic infections may occur as a result of contamination of fractures or following orthopaedic surgery
D. F   it survives best in moist environments
E. F   vancomycin is not active against Gram-negative organisms

A116.

A. F   but dosage should be reduced in severe renal impairment
B. T
C. F   but levels should be measured in neonates and infants
D. T
E. F

A117.
A. F
B. F   prolonged antibiotic therapy alone is sufficient unless there is significant bronchial obstruction
C. T   right-sided endocarditis or acute osteomyelitis is often the source
D. T   more than one organism (including anaerobes) may be involved
E. T

A118.
A. T
B. T
C. T
D. F   multiple organisms are often involved, some of which may be resistant to ampicillin
E. T

A119.
A. F   this remains fully sensitive to penicillin
B. T   penicillin resistance is now common in many parts of the world
C. T   multiple antibiotic resistance is common in many countries
D. T   though still uncommon, resistance to penicillin is increasing
E. T   as in C

A120.
A. F   resistance is known to occur, particularly after long-term treatment
B. F   two types, HSV1 and HSV2, are recognised
C. T   HSV2 is more commonly associated with genital herpes
D. T
E. F   though perinatal infection may occur in the neonate

A121.
A. T
B. T
C. T   the natural host is the rat
D. F   transmission is by fleas
E. F   is endemic in wild rodent populations in many countries

A122.

A. T   usually as tropical pyomyositis
B. F   though myositis is common, it is not a cause of pyogenic lesions
C. T   localised muscle necrosis and abscesses are a rare but well recognised complication of enteric fever
D. F
E. F   though myositis is a common feature, abscess formation does not occur

A123.

A. F   PCR detects specific DNA sequences, not antibodies
B. F   PCR-based tests take several hours
C. T
D. F   specific DNA sequences remain detectable long after death
E. T   though still mainly a research tool, it may prove useful in routine diagnosis in the future

A124.

A. T   an increasingly important cause of acute haemorrhagic colitis
B. F   mainly affects the ileum
C. T   causes pseudomembranous colitis
D. T   causes bacillary dysentery
E. F   this is a non-pathogenic species; the pathogenic species of intestinal amoeba is *Entamoeba histolytica*

A125.

A. T
B. T
C. F   chlorhexidine is effective but does not guarantee the complete elimination of HIV
D. T
E. T

A126.

A. F *Staphylococcus aureus* is often carried as a commensal in many sites, e.g. nose, throat, skin

B. F latent infection and occasional excretion in body fluids occurs in many asymptomatic patients

C. F many normal persons, especially the elderly or the very young, may asymptomatically excrete this organism in their stools

D. T

E. F faecal excretion of cysts often continues after recovery from the acute colitis

A127.

A. T

B. T but uneconomic for this purpose

C. T

D. T

E. F as in B; autoclaving is preferred

A128.

A. T

B. T

C. T

D. T

E. T

A129.

A. T these include Ebola, Marburg and Lassa viruses

B. T malaria should be excluded as soon as possible

C. F if VHF is suspected, routine laboratory tests should be delayed until this diagnosis is excluded by the reference virus laboratory

D. T but in addition to marking specimens appropriately, close liaison with the laboratory and infectious disease specialists is necessary

E. T if VHF is confirmed or strongly suspected, isolation in special isolation units is necessary

A130.
A. T
B. T   *Candida albicans* is the most common yeast; the other main pathogen causing oesophagitis is herpes simplex virus
C. T   the presence of oesophagitis is often associated with disseminated infection
D. F   oesophageal infection is usually confined to the mucosa
E. F   aetiological diagnosis requires oesophagoscopy and biopsy for microbiological investigation

A131.
A. T   severe cases may show marked oedema and bullae
B. T
C. F   caused by *Streptococcus pyogenes*, even though it is often difficult to isolate the organism from the lesion
D. T
E. F   this feature is characteristic of shingles (varicella zoster infection) rather than erysipelas

A132.
A. F   diagnosis is on the basis of the characteristic clinical features
B. T   but retrograde spread along peripheral nerve axons is the more important route
C. T   this is an important cause of death in patients who are managed by the total paralysis regimen
D. T   human antitetanus globulin is useful for immediate protection after tetanus-prone injury, but long term protection is best provided by active immunisation with tetanus toxoid
E. T

A133.
A. T   pyogenic abscesses in the thyroid are rare but well recognised
B. T   de Quervain's thyroiditis is thought to be of viral aetiology
C. T   but this is usually self-limiting
D. F   bacterial infection in the thyroid is rare and localised
E. F

A134.
A. T
B. F spores are not stained by the Gram's method and appear as clear areas
C. F spores stay dormant during adverse conditions
D. T antibiotics act by interfering with bacterial metabolic pathways and so cannot affect the dormant spores
E. T they are formed only by Gram-positive genera such as *Clostridium* and *Bacillus*

A135.
A. T
B. T may code for virulence factors such as toxin production
C. T
D. T are sometimes transmissible between related species
E. F plasmids are composed of bacterial DNA

A136.
A. F diagnosis is by microscopy of stool samples or jejunal aspirates
B. T cysts are found in faecally contaminated water supplies
C. F
D. F affects mainly the duodenum and jejunum
E. T

A137.
A. T
B. F not a protozoon
C. T this is a flagellate protozoon
D. F as in B
E. T

A138.
A. F but prevalence is higher in older age groups in developed countries
B. F infection is transmitted by close contact, e.g. by saliva
C. T this forms the basis of the breath test, which detects ammonia release after ingestion of urea substrate
D. T
E. T but relapse or reinfection may occur

A139.
A. F
B. T
C. F   *Mycoplasma pneumoniae* is a common cause, not *Mycoplasma hominis*
D. T
E. T

A140.
A. F   mumps parotitis is usually bilateral
B. T
C. T   duct obstruction, often due to calculi, is often complicated by pyogenic infection
D. F   but pyogenic infection may require antibiotic therapy in addition to the removal of any obstruction
E. F   neoplasms in the parotid gland are generally slow-growing

A141.
A. T   due to *Chlamydia trachomatis* serotypes D–K
B. T   due to *Chlamydia pneumoniae*
C. T   due to *Chlamydia trachomatis* serotypes A–C
D. F   these conditions are associated with *Helicobacter pylori*
E. T   due to *Chlamydia trachomatis* serotypes L1, L2 and L3

A142.
A. F   the colonising organisms are mostly Gram-positive, e.g. *Staphylococcus epidermidis*
B. T   known as "shunt nephritis", due to immune complex deposition
C. T
D. T
E. T

A143.
A. F
B. F   blood cultures are often negative in disseminated candidiasis
C. T   this is a rare but important long term complication
D. T
E. T   dissemination is often preceded by colonisation in multiple sites

A144.

A. T   pyogenic liver abscesses are often due to mixed infections including anaerobes
B. T   similar to A
C. F
D. F   infection is usually due to penicillin-sensitive organisms such as *Streptococcus pneumoniae* or *Streptococcus pyogenes*
E. F   single agents effective against Gram-positive organisms are adequate

A145.

A. F   though myocarditis may occur in diphtheria, due to blood-borne exotoxin
B. T
C. T
D. F   many strains of this organism are non-toxigenic
E. F   culture is essential for specific diagnosis; staining methods are not sufficiently discriminatory

A146.

A. T
B. F
C. T
D. F
E. T

A147.

A. T   but the organism has not been grown on tissue culture
B. F   infection affects the stratum corneum
C. F   the immune response is often ineffective and variable
D. F   though some members of this family of viruses are associated with malignancy, e.g. carcinoma of the cervix, plantar or common skin warts are not
E. T

A148.
A. T uncommon, but important
B. T often secondary to sinusitis or otitis media
C. T not uncommon as a complication of pneumococcal septicaemia
D. T often secondary to lobar pneumonia
E. T uncommon and often unrecognised unless strains are serotyped

A149.
A. T
B. T
C. F only some third-generation cephalosporins, e.g. ceftazidime, have good activity against *Pseudomonas* spp
D. F this antibiotic has activity against Gram-positive organisms
E. T

A150.
A. T
B. F obligate anaerobes are by far the most common organisms in the colon
C. F
D. T particularly in the neonatal period
E. T verotoxin-positive *Escherichia coli* (VTEC), such as *Escherichia coli* O-157, are responsible

Section 4   Questions

151. Ischiorectal abscesses

A. are most commonly due to infection with *Staphylococcus aureus*
B. are a complication in patients with neutropenia
C. require the bacteriological culture of the pus and sensitivity testing of organisms for optimal treatment
D. recur usually due to infection with antibiotic-resistant organisms
E. may lead to septicaemia

152. The following is/are true of Epstein–Barr virus

A. it is a herpesvirus
B. it causes hepatitis
C. it is associated with lymphoma
D. it is susceptible to treatment with acyclovir
E. it is a cause of severe sore throat

153. Infection of closed CSF shunts installed for the relief of hydrocephalus

A. presents with swinging pyrexia
B. is mostly due to skin organisms such as *Staphylococcus epidermidis* or diphtheroids
C. may be diagnosed by positive blood cultures
D. results in nephritis due to haematogenous spread of infection to the kidneys
E. can often be successfully eradicated with intraventricular administration of antibiotics

154. The following organisms may cause disease primarily mediated by exotoxins

A. *Clostridium perfringens*
B. *Bacillus cereus*
C. *Escherichia coli*
D. *Salmonella typhi*
E. *Clostridium botulinum*

155. The following is/are true of tuberculosis

A. most new cases in western countries are among immigrants
B. immunity is mainly cell-mediated
C. infection in childhood leaves long-lasting immunity
D. bone infection is usually treated with chemotherapy alone
E. laboratory culture and sensitivity tests may take several weeks to complete

156. Diseases associated with *Clostridium perfringens* include

A. pseudomembranous colitis
B. necrotising enterocolitis
C. gas gangrene
D. food poisoning
E. necrotising fasciitis

157. The following antimicrobial agents are rapidly absorbed and systemically effective after oral administration

A. metronidazole
B. vancomycin
C. acyclovir
D. neomycin
E. amphotericin B

158. Pathogens that cause cervical lymphadenopathy in children include

A. *Mycobacterium avium-intracellulare*
B. *Toxoplasma gondii*
C. rubella virus
D. mumps virus
E. *Mycobacterium tuberculosis*

159. Splenomegaly is a feature of

A. hepatitis A infection
B. malaria
C. typhoid
D. infectious mononucleosis
E. schistosomiasis

160. Lipid A, responsible for the biological activity of Gram-negative endotoxin

A. is found in the inner layer of the bacterial cell wall
B. is found in the cell membrane
C. shows great variation in chemical structure between different species of Gram-negative bacilli
D. induces the production of tumour necrosis factor in macrophages
E. acts as a strong antigen and elicits protective antibody responses in the host

161. Organisms causing infections in the ileum include

A. *Mycobacterium tuberculosis*
B. *Shigella dysenteriae*
C. *Salmonella typhi*
D. *rotavirus*
E. *Clostridium perfringens*

162. The formation of resistant spores or cysts is important in the spread of infections due to the following organisms

A. *Clostridium difficile*
B. *Cryptosporidium* spp
C. *Pseudomonas aeruginosa*
D. *Giardia lamblia*
E. *Strongyloides stercoralis*

163. Cytomegalovirus infection

A. occurs mostly in immunocompromised patients
B. may present with generalised lymphadenopathy
C. is usually diagnosed by virus isolation
D. requires specific antiviral therapy when clinical disease is present
E. may be complicated by severe enterocolitis

164. Organisms found as part of the commensal flora of the skin include

A. *Escherichia coli*
B. *Staphylococcus aureus*
C. *Corynebacterium* spp
D. *Candida albicans*
E. α-haemolytic streptococci

165. Urine is an important route for transmission of infection in

A. syphilis
B. schistosomiasis
C. acute glomerulonephritis
D. tuberculosis
E. leptospirosis

166. Saliva is a common vehicle for the transmission of

A. Epstein–Barr virus
B. mumps
C. herpes simplex
D. *Shigella* spp
E. cytomegalovirus

167. Causative agents of septic arthritis include

A. *Neisseria gonorrhoeae*
B. *Streptococcus pneumoniae*
C. *Shigella dysenteriae*
D. *Haemophilus influenzae*
E. *Staphylococcus aureus*

168. The following factors predispose to urinary tract infection

A. urinary catheterisation
B. pregnancy
C. diabetes mellitus
D. uterine prolapse
E. previous urinary tract infection

169. **"Significant bacteriuria" is generally considered to be 10^5 organisms/ml in a mid-stream urine sample. Lower numbers may however be considered significant in samples obtained from**

A. catheter drainage bags
B. suprapubic aspiration
C. sampling ports in closed drainage urinary catheters
D. nephrostomy tubes
E. "bag urine" from babies

170. **Common sources of infection during prosthetic joint implantation surgery include**

A. inadequately sterilised instruments
B. dust particles from the operating theatre air
C. blood-borne infections from colonic or mouth flora
D. patient's skin
E. surgeon's hands

171. **The most reliable finding in surgical wound infection is**

A. isolation of a pathogenic organism
B. oedema
C. redness
D. presence of purulent discharge
E. fever

172. **Hand-washing is essential in preventing cross-infections with**

A. *Staphylococcus aureus*
B. common cold viruses
C. *Mycobacterium tuberculosis*
D. *Streptococcus pyogenes*
E. *Klebsiella pneumoniae*

173. Aerobic Gram-positive bacilli include

A. *Actinomyces* spp
B. *Bacillus anthracis*
C. *Listeria* spp
D. *Clostridium difficile*
E. *Legionella pneumophila*

174. *Klebsiella pneumoniae*

A. is a Gram-negative bacillus
B. causes lobar pneumonia
C. is usually sensitive to ampicillin
D. is a common cause of wound infection
E. may cause hospital cross-infection

175. Scarlet fever

A. may accompany streptococcal infection of surgical wounds
B. may be caused by all strains of β-haemolytic streptococci
C. is now rarely seen in the UK
D. treatment with penicillin shortens the duration of the rash
E. diagnosis may be confirmed by serological tests for antistreptolysin O antibodies

176. Infection caused by a penicillinase-producing, cloxacillin-susceptible *Staphylococcus aureus* may be treated with

A. ampicillin
B. co-amoxiclav
C. cefuroxime
D. phenoxymethylpenicillin
E. metronidazole

177. Diarrhoea with blood and mucus may be caused by

A. *Clostridium difficile*
B. verotoxin-producing strains of *Escherichia coli*
C. *Vibrio cholerae*
D. *Campylobacter jejuni*
E. *Giardia lamblia*

178. Jaundice is often a feature of

A. amoebic liver abscess
B. vivax malaria
C. typhoid fever
D. leptospirosis
E. hepatitis A infection

179. Liver abscesses

A. are often multiple
B. are more common in patients with biliary obstruction
C. may be diagnosed by serological tests
D. require surgical drainage as part of their management
E. may lead to metastatic abscesses

180. In pulmonary nocardiosis

A. the causative organisms are fungi related to *Aspergillus* spp
B. Gram stain of the sputum sample is often diagnostic
C. metastatic infection is common
D. a prolonged course of penicillin is usually curative
E. blood cultures may be positive

181. In acute bacterial prostatitis

A. the common causative organisms are coliforms
B. the aetiological diagnosis is confirmed by culture of the urine
C. chronic prostatitis is a common complication
D. treatment with antibiotics is often effective
E. blood cultures may be positive

182. Immunoglobulins of the IgM class

A. are the earliest to be produced in an immune response
B. may be found in foetal blood as a result of transfer across the placenta
   from maternal blood
C. are associated with anaphylactic (type 1) hypersensitivity
D. are poor activators of complement
E. constitute 30%–40% of total immunoglobulins

183. Gram-negative cocci found as human pathogens or commensals include

A. *Enterococcus faecalis*
B. *Moraxella (Branhamella) catarrhalis*
C. *Neisseria meningitidis*
D. *Haemophilus influenzae*
E. *Cryptosporidium* spp

184. The following is/are true of metronidazole

A. is absorbed well when given orally
B. is safe in pregnancy
C. is active against many protozoan parasites
D. is contra-indicated in renal insufficiency
E. does not cross the blood–brain barrier well

185. Stevens–Johnson syndrome

A. may be associated with penicillin therapy
B. can occur in herpes simplex infection
C. manifests as maculopapular lesions on the skin
D. is a complication of infection with *Mycoplasma pneumoniae*
E. is an example of cell-mediated hypersensitivity

186. In mumps

A. the causative agent may be isolated from the urine
B. vaccination is ineffective because of the antigenic diversity among strains of the causative virus
C. bilateral parotitis is a characteristic clinical feature
D. specific therapy is not required
E. serological tests are of value in confirming the diagnosis

187. Vincent's angina

A. is associated with mixed anaerobic infection
B. is spread from person to person by infected secretions
C. may be diagnosed by examination of a Gram-stained preparation of infected tissue or exudate
D. is more common in granulocytopenic patients
E. requires treatment with broad spectrum antibiotics

188. Infections characterised by colitis are caused by

A. *Giardia lamblia*
B. *Entamoeba coli*
C. *Helicobacter pylori*
D. *Escherichia coli* serotype O-157
E. *Salmonella enteritidis*

189. Antibiotics useful in the treatment of pseudomembranous colitis include

A. fluoroquinolones such as ciprofloxacin
B. vancomycin
C. co-amoxiclav
D. tetracyclines
E. metronidazole

190. Brucellosis

A. may present as epididymo-orchitis
B. may be spread by the inhalation of infected aerosols
C. can have an incubation period of many months
D. is often diagnosed by a positive blood culture
E. is localised in the tissues of the reticuloendothelial system

191. Infections in which *Candida albicans* may be an aetiological agent are

A. suppurative peripheral thrombophlebitis
B. endophthalmitis
C. pneumonia
D. endocarditis
E. peritonitis

192. Pancreatitis is a recognised complication in infections with

A. coxsackie B virus
B. hepatitis C virus
C. mumps
D. cytomegalovirus
E. chicken pox

193. The following organisms cause chronic infections of the urinary bladder

A. *Giardia lamblia*
B. *Entamoeba histolytica*
C. *Schistosoma haematobium*
D. *Mycobacterium tuberculosis*
E. *Candida albicans*

194. Intra-abdominal infections in the right iliac fossa region are associated with

A. *Bacteroides fragilis*
B. *Helicobacter pylori*
C. *Entamoeba histolytica*
D. *Giardia lamblia*
E. *Yersinia enterocolitica*

195. β-haemolytic streptococcus group B

A. is also known as *Streptococcus agalactiae*
B. causes endocarditis
C. is associated with urinary tract infections
D. causes meningitis
E. is usually resistant to penicillin

196. Useful specimens for the aetiological diagnosis of acute osteomyelitis are

A. pus from needle aspiration or surgical drainage
B. throat swab
C. clotted blood for serology
D. nose swab
E. blood for culture

197. Serum complement

A. causes lysis of bacteria
B. is composed of three serum proteins
C. receptors for the active components are found on red blood cells
D. does not play a significant role in phagocytosis
E. plays a key role in type 1 (anaphylactic) hypersensitivity

198. Spirochaetes include

A. *Borrelia burgdorferi*
B. *Leptospira icterohaemorrhagiae*
C. *Brucella abortus*
D. *Bacteroides fragilis*
E. *Treponema pallidum*

199. Interleukins

A. are only active locally, as signal molecules between leucocytes
B. may be produced by non-lymphoid cells
C. have immunological specificity in their action
D. have all been chemically characterised
E. may show direct cytotoxicity against virus-infected cells

200. Immunoglobulins of the IgE class

A. constitute 1%–10% of total immunoglobulins in normal serum
B. activate complement after specific reaction with antigens
C. cross the placenta in significant amounts
D. cause degranulation of mast cells and basophils after reaction with specific antigens
E. play a protective role in parasitic infections

Section 4   Answers

A151.
A. F   infections are most often due to faecal organisms such as coliforms and anaerobes
B. T   though most of these abscesses occur in immunocompetent individuals, severely neutropenic patients are liable to abscesses and spreading cellulitis in the perianal region
C. F   incision and drainage are adequate in most cases
D. F   antibiotic resistance is rarely a reason for recurrence
E. F   except in the severely immunocompromised

A152.
A. T
B. T
C. T   Burkitt's lymphoma, seen mainly in west Africa
D. F
E. T   seen in glandular fever

A153.
A. F   presents with low grade pyrexia
B. T
C. T
D. F   nephritis does occur, but it is immune-complex mediated
E. F   infection may be controlled, but eradication with antibiotics is difficult to achieve

A154.
A. T
B. T   the enterotoxin causes the food poisoning associated with this organism
C. T   some strains produce potent exotoxins, such as the verotoxin produced by *Escherichia coli* O-157
D. F   this organism causes disease by tissue invasion
E. T

A155.

A. F though the incidence is relatively high among immigrants, particularly within the first five years of immigration, the majority of cases in terms of absolute numbers still occur in the native population

B. T

C. F infection often remains dormant and may become active in later life

D. T surgery is now rarely required

E. T

A156.

A. F pseudomembranous colitis is caused by toxigenic strains of *Clostridium difficile*

B. T

C. T

D. T

E. F necrotising fasciitis is caused most commonly by *Streptococcus pyogenes*, though other organisms may also be involved

A157.

A. T

B. F the oral preparation is intended to be active only in the gut lumen, e.g. when used for the treatment of pseudomembranous colitis

C. T

D. F as in B

E. F as in B

A158.

A. T

B. T

C. T characteristically in the occipital region

D. F

E. T but in developed countries, cervical lymphadenopathy is more commonly due to atypical mycobacteria, e.g. *Mycobacterium avium-intracellulare*.

A159.

A. F

B. T though the splenic enlargement may be minimal or clinically undetectable in the early stages.

C. T as in B

D. T present in nearly half the patients

E. T due to both portal hypertension and chronic immunological stimulation

A160.

A. T

B. F

C. F

D. T

E. F

A161.

A. T

B. F this is a cause of acute colitis

C. T

D. T

E. F as in B

A162.

A. T this is also true of other clostridial pathogens

B. T cysts are resistant to water purification methods

C. F this organism does not produce spores or cysts

D. T as in B

E. F infection is due to skin penetration by larvae

A163.

A. F it is a common infection in the normal population, but severe infection occurs in the immunocompromised

B. T

C. F serology is the main method of diagnosis, although culture is possible

D. F but severe infection in the immunocompromised, such as retinitis, can be treated with ganciclovir or foscarnet

E. T in the immunocompromised

A164.

A. F although transient carriage may occur, especially in the perineal area

B. T but far less common than coagulase-negative staphylococci such as *Staphylococcus epidermidis*

C. T commonly known as "diphtheroids"

D. F though transient carriage may occur

E. F these are commensals of the mouth and upper respiratory tract

A165.

A. F though a sexually transmitted disease, viable organisms are rarely found in urine

B. T eggs are excreted in the urine or faeces of infected persons

C. F acute glomerulonephritis is usually an immunological consequence of streptococcal throat or skin infection

D. F though organisms are excreted in urine in genitourinary tuberculosis, urine is rarely the source of infection

E. T often from zoonotic (animal) contamination of streams, canals, sewers, etc.

A166.

A. T

B. T

C. T

D. F transmission is faeco-oral

E. T

A167.

A. T

B. T

C. F though an arthritic syndrome (Reiter's syndrome) may occasionally follow dysentery, there is no infection of the joints

D. T particularly in children, though this is becoming rare following the introduction of *Haemophilus influenzae* type B (HIB) vaccine

E. T the most common cause of pyogenic arthritis in all age groups

A168.
A. T
B. T
C. T
D. T
E. T

A169.
A. F   these are often contaminated
B. T
C. T
D. T
E. F   often contaminated with perineal organisms

A170.
A. F   failure of instrument sterilisation is a rare occurrence
B. T   these particles are mainly skin squames from operating room personnel
C. F   though possible, this source is uncommon in early postoperative infections
D. T   but less common than B
E. F

A171.
A. F   bacterial cultures do not consistently yield growth of the pathogenic organisms
B. F   infection is not the only cause of oedema in surgical wounds
C. F   as in B
D. T
E. F   as in B

A172.
A. T
B. T   spread by contact may be more important than droplet spread
C. F   spread is airborne
D. T
E. T

A173.
A. T these are branching Gram-positive rods
B. T
C. T
D. F though this is a Gram-positive rod, it is a strict anaerobe
E. F this is a Gram-negative rod

A174.
A. T
B. T but this is an uncommon cause, usually as a consequence of aspiration
C. F cephalosporins or aminoglycosides are more effective
D. F but may cause hospital-acquired infection particularly of urinary catheters, intravenous lines, etc.
E. T see D

A175.
A. T
B. F due to some strains of *Streptococcus pyogenes*
C. T
D. F
E. T

A176.
A. F ampicillin is as susceptible to the action of staphylococcal β-lactamase as is penicillin
B. T the clavulanic acid component of co-amoxiclav blocks the action of the staphylococcal β-lactamase
C. T cefuroxime is not susceptible to the action of the staphylococcal β-lactamase
D. F as in A
E. F metronidazole has no activity against any strains of staphylococci

A177.

Note: Infective diarrhoea with blood and mucus is usually a feature of colitis, but not of enteritis.

A. T
B. T
C. F   this is exclusively an enteritis causing profuse watery diarrhoea
D. T   though not a common presentation, severe cases can present with blood and mucus
E. F   infection is confined to the duodenum and jejunum

A178.

A. F   amoebic liver abscesses are localised and rarely cause jaundice
B. T   due to haemolysis of parasitised red cells
C. F   though, rarely, hepatic involvement may be sufficient to cause jaundice
D. T   most cases are mild or anicteric, but 5%–10% of cases may present with jaundice
E. T

A179.

Note: Liver abscesses may be pyogenic (due to bacteria, often of gut origin and mixed) or amoebic (secondary to colitis due to *Entamoeba histolytica*).

A. T   particularly in pyogenic abscesses secondary to biliary obstruction
B. T   multiple pyogenic liver abscesses are a complication of biliary obstruction
C. T   amoebic liver abscesses may be diagnosed by serological tests
D. F   most liver abscesses can be managed by appropriate antibiotic therapy alone
E. T   spread by direct extension or bacteraemic spread, e.g. to the brain, are recognised complications

A190.
A. T
B. T
C. T
D. T   blood culture is a sensitive and specific diagnostic procedure, but special media and prolonged culture are needed
E. F   infection can affect many organ systems

A191.
A. T   associated with colonisation of an intravenous line
B. T
C. F   candida pneumonia is not a well recognised clinical entity, but diffuse pneumonitis may occur as part of disseminated candidiasis
D. T   rare but important
E. T   often associated with peritoneal dialysis

A192.
A. T
B. F
C. T
D. F
E. F

A193.
A. F
B. F
C. T
D. T
E. T

A194.
A. T
B. F   infection due to this organism is usually confined to the stomach
C. T
D. F
E. T

A195.

A. T
B. T uncommon but serious cause
C. T as in B
D. T particularly in neonates
E. F

A196.

A. T
B. F
C. F
D. F
E. T blood culture is nearly always positive in acute osteomyelitis

A197.

A. T
B. F more than 30 component proteins are recognised within the complement system
C. T receptors are also found on other cells, such as phagocytes and macrophages
D. F opsonisation with specific antibody and complement is a pre-requisite for phagocytosis of many bacteria
E. F

A198.

A. T
B. T
C. F this is a Gram-negative rod
D. F as in C
E. T

A199.

A. **F**   though their most important role is to act as local modulators of the immune response, some interleukins have systemic activity, e.g. as pyrogens or as bone marrow stimulants

B. **T**   though most interleukins are produced by T lymphocytes, other cell types, such as macrophage-monocytes and endothelial cells, also produce some interleukins

C. **F**

D. **T**   only those cytokines that have been fully characterised are designated as interleukins (e.g. IL-1, IL-2, etc.)

E. **F**   interleukins have no direct cytotoxic activity, but they modulate the cytotoxicity of other effector cells

A200.

A. **F**   IgE constitutes less than 0.01% of normal serum immuno-globulins

B. **F**   but the alternate pathway (i.e. not dependent on specific antigen–antibody reactions) may be activated by IgE aggregates

C. **F**   only IgG crosses the placenta in significant amounts

D. **T**

E. **T**   this is particularly true of helminths